THE ŠIKSHÂ-PATRÎ
of the
SVÂMI-NÂRÂYANA SECT

JOURNAL OF THE ROYAL ASIATIC SOCIETY.

By

SIR MONIER MONIER-WILLIAMS

First published in 1882

This edition published by Read Books Ltd.
Copyright © 2019 Read Books Ltd.
This book is copyright and may not be
reproduced or copied in any way without
the express permission of the publisher in writing

British Library Cataloguing-in-Publication Data
A catalogue record for this book is available
from the British Library

ORIGIN AND GROWTH OF HINDUISM

AN EXCERPT FROM INDUISM AND BUDDHISM
AN HISTORICAL SKETCH
BY
SIR CHARLES ELIOT.

The earliest product of Indian literature, the Rig Veda, contains the songs of the Aryan invaders who were beginning to make a home in India. Though no longer nomads, they had little local sentiment. No cities had arisen comparable with Babylon or Thebes and we hear little of ancient kingdoms or dynasties. Many of the gods who occupied so much of their thoughts were personifications of natural forces such as the sun, wind and fire, worshipped without temples or images and hence more indefinite in form, habitation and attributes than the deities of Assyria or Egypt. The idea of a struggle between good and evil was not prominent. In Persia, where the original pantheon was almost the same as that of the Veda, this idea produced monotheism: the minor deities became angels and the chief deity a Lord of hosts who wages a successful struggle against an independent but still inferior spirit of evil. But in India the Spirits of Good and Evil are not thus personified. The world is regarded less as a battlefield of principles than as a theatre for the display of natural forces. No one god assumes lordship over the others but all are seen to be interchangeable—mere names and aspects of something which is greater than any god.

Indian religion is commonly regarded as the offspring of an Aryan religion, brought into India by invaders from the north and modified by contact with Dravidian civilization. The materials at our disposal hardly permit us to take any other point of view, for the literature of the Vedic Aryans is relatively ancient and full and we have no information about the old Dravidians comparable with it. But were our knowledge less one-sided, we might see that it would be more correct to describe Indian religion as Dravidian religion stimulated and modified by the ideas of Aryan invaders. For the greatest deities of Hinduism, Siva, Krishna, Râma, Durgâ and some of its most essential doctrines such as metempsychosis and divine incarnations, are either totally unknown to the Veda or obscurely adumbrated in it. The chief characteristics of mature Indian religion are characteristics of an area, not of a race, and they are not the characteristics of religion in Persia, Greece or other Aryan lands.

Some writers explain Indian religion as the worship of nature spirits, others as the veneration of the dead. But it is a mistake to see in the religion of any large area only one origin or impulse. The principles which in a learned form are championed to-day by various professors represent thoughts which were creative in early times. In ancient India there were some whose minds turned to their ancestors and dead friends while others saw divinity in the wonders of storm, spring and harvest. Krishna is in the main a product of hero worship, but Śiva has no such historical basis. He personifies the powers of birth and death, of change, decay and rebirth—in fact all that we include in the prosaic word nature. Assuredly both these lines of thought—the worship of nature and of the dead—and perhaps many others existed in ancient India.

By the time of the Upanishads, that is about 600 B.C., we trace three clear currents in Indian religion which have persisted until the present day. The first is ritual. This became extraordinarily complicated but retained its primitive and magical character. The object of an ancient Indian sacrifice was partly to please the gods but still more to coerce them by certain acts and formulae. Secondly all Hindus lay stress on asceticism and self-mortification, as a means of purifying the soul and obtaining supernatural powers. They have a conviction that every man who is in earnest about religion and even every student of philosophy must follow a discipline at least to the extent of observing chastity and eating only to support life. Severer austerities give clearer insight into divine mysteries and control over the forces of nature. Europeans are apt to condemn eastern asceticism as a waste of life but it has had an important moral effect. The weakness of Hinduism, though not of Buddhism, is that ethics have so small a place in its fundamental conceptions. Its deities are not identified with the moral law and the saint is above that law. But this dangerous doctrine is corrected by the dogma, which is also a popular conviction, that a saint must be a passionless ascetic. In India no religious teacher can expect a hearing unless he begins by renouncing the world.

Thirdly, the deepest conviction of Hindus in all ages is that salvation and happiness are attainable by knowledge. The corresponding phrases in Sanskrit are perhaps less purely intellectual than our word and contain some idea of effort and emotion. He who knows God attains to God, nay he is God. Rites and self-denial are but necessary preliminaries to such knowledge: he who possesses it stands above them. It is inconceivable to the Hindus that he should care for the things of the world but he cares equally little for creeds and ceremonies. Hence, side by side with irksome codes, complicated ritual and elaborate theology, we find the conviction that all these things are but vanity and weariness, fetters to be shaken off by the free in spirit. Nor do those who hold such views correspond to the anti-clerical and radical parties of Europe. The ascetic sitting in the temple court often holds that the rites performed around him are spiritually useless and the gods of the shrine mere fanciful presentments of that which cannot be depicted or described.

Rather later, but still before the Christian era, another idea makes itself prominent in Indian religion, namely faith or devotion to a particular deity. This idea, which needs no explanation, is pushed on the one hand to every extreme of theory and practice: on the other it rarely abolishes altogether the belief in ritualism, asceticism and knowledge.

Any attempt to describe Hinduism as one whole leads to startling contrasts. The same religion enjoins self-mortification and orgies: commands human sacrifices and yet counts it a sin to eat meat or crush an insect: has more priests, rites and images than ancient Egypt or medieval Rome and yet out does Quakers in rejecting all externals. These singular features are connected with the ascendancy of the Brahman caste. The Brahmans are an interesting social phenomenon without exact parallel elsewhere. They are not, like the Catholic or Moslem clergy, a priesthood pledged to support certain doctrines but an intellectual, hereditary aristocracy who claim to direct the thought of India whatever forms it may take. All who admit this claim and accord a nominal recognition to the authority of the Veda are within the spacious fold or menagerie. Neither the devil-worshipping aboriginee nor the atheistic philosopher is excommunicated, though neither may be relished by average orthodoxy.

hough Hinduism has no one creed, yet there are at least two doctrines held by nearly all who call themselves Hindus. One may be described as polytheistic pantheism. Most Hindus are apparently polytheists, that is to say they venerate the images of several deities or spirits, yet most are monotheists in the sense that they address their worship to one god. But this monotheism has almost always a pantheistic tinge. The Hindu does not say the gods of the heathen are but idols, but it is the Lord who made the heavens: he says, My Lord (Râma, Krishna or whoever it may be) is all the other gods. Some schools would prefer to say that no human language applied to the Godhead can be correct and that all ideas of a personal ruler of the world are at best but relative truths. This ultimate ineffable Godhead is called Brahman.

The second doctrine is commonly known as metempsychosis, the transmigration of souls or reincarnation, the last name being the most correct. In detail the doctrine assumes various forms since different views are held about the relation of soul to body. But the essence of all is the same, namely that a life does not begin at birth or end at death but is a link in an infinite series of lives, each of which is conditioned and determined by the acts done in previous existences (karma). Animal, human and divine (or at least angelic) existences may all be links in the chain. A man's deeds, if good, may exalt him to the heavens, if evil may degrade him to life as a beast. Since all lives, even in heaven, must come to an end, happiness is not to be sought in heaven or on earth. The common aspiration of the religious Indian is for deliverance, that is release from the round of births and repose in some changeless state called by such names as union with Brahman, nirvana and many others.

ART. XXIV.--*Sanskrit Text of the Šikshâ-Patrî of the Svâmi-Nârâyana Sect.* Edited by Professor Monier Williams, C.I.E., D.C.L.

THE text of the Šikshâ-Patrî of the modern Vaishnava Sect, called Svâmi-Nârâyana, was lithographed in Samvat 1928 (A.D. 1872) by order of the Heads of the Sect. It has a Gujarâtî Commentary by Nityânanda-muni. So far as I know, this is the only version of the text that has yet appeared. It was given to me by the Wartâl Mahârâja on the occasion of my first visit to Wartâl in 1875. It is full of mistakes, and in preparing the following edition of the text I have taken as my guide the far more accurate manuscript and Sanskrit commentary written by Pan.dit Šatânanda-muni, and given to me by the Mahârâja on the same occasion.

THE ŠIKSHÂ-PATRÎ OF THE SVÂMI-NÂRÂYANA SECT

TRANSLATION OF THE FOREGOING ŠIKSHÂ-PATRÎ. BY PROFESSOR MONIER WILLIAMS.

In making the following translation I have been careful to study the Sanskrit commentary called Artha-dîpikâ, written for me in clear beautiful characters by Pandit Šatânanda-muni (one of the disciples of Svâmi-Nârâyana), by order of the Wartâl Mahârâja, after one of the formal visits to the Wartâl Temple, which were kindly arranged for me by Mr. Frederick Sheppard, C.S., late Collector of Kaira, and now Commissioner. The translation is the first ever made by any European scholar, though it is right I should mention that I have consulted a fairly accurate version (not always perfect either in its renderings or its English) written by Sheth Bhogilâl Prânjîvandâs, of the Bombay Education Society's Institution, Ahmedabad, and given in Mr. H. C. Briggs' work, "The Cities of Gujarâshtra." I have also received assistance from my friend Pan.dit Shyâmajî Krishna-varmâ, of Balliol College, Oxford.

1. I meditate in my heart on that Krishna on whose left side is seated Râdhâ, on whose breast reclines Šrî (Lakshmî), and who enjoyed sport (with them) in V.rindâvana.

2. I, Sahajânandah Svâmî (afterwards called Svâmî-Nârâyana), living at Vrittâlaya, write this Letter of instructions (or Book of directions) to all my followers scattered throughout various countries.

3. Let the two youths named Ayodhyâ-prasâda and Raghu-vîra, the sons of my two brothers, Râma-pratâpa and Içchâ-râma,

who were the children of Dharma (or Hari-prasâda);

4. And let those Naishthika Brahmaçârîs (that is to say, those Brahmans who continue Brahma-çârîs or celibates all their lives), the chief among whom is Mukundânanda, and those Grihasthas (householders), such as Mayârâma-Bhatta, and other of my followers;

5. And let those women, whether wives or widows, who have become my disciples, and the whole number of holy men (Sâdhus), such as Muktânanda and others;

6. Let all these (persons) constantly give heed to my prayers for their perpetual continuance in their own proper duties--(my prayers) offered up with repetition of the name Krishna (Nârâyana), and in accordance with the sacred scriptures. (Literally--Let my benedictory words which keep them in their own duties be always read by all these persons accompanied by repetition of the name of Krishna, and approved by the Šâstras.)

7. Let this Letter of directions, which has important objects (to be hereafter enumerated), and which promotes the welfare of all living beings, be studied with perfect concentration of mind by all these (persons).

8. Those (virtuous) persons who conform to the good usages enjoined by the sacred Šâstras will always enjoy great happiness both in this world and in that which is to come.

9. But those evil-minded persons who wilfully transgress such (good usages) will certainly suffer great misery in this world as well as in the next.

10. Therefore let all of you who are my disciples always remain careful and well-contented in the observance of this (Book of

directions).

11. Let no followers of mine ever intentionally kill any living thing whatever--not even a louse, flea, or the most minute insect.

12. The killing of any animal such as a goat, etc., for the purpose of sacrificing to the Gods and Pitris, must not be practised; because it is declared, that abstinence from injury to others is the highest of all duties.

13. The killing of any human being in any way, at any place, for any object, (even) for the sake of acquiring a wife, wealth, or political supremacy, is wholly prohibited.

14. Suicide at a sacred place of pilgrimage, or from passion, either by hanging, or by poison in consequence of the commission of a criminal act [Footnote: A father sometimes kills himself because a criminal act has been committed by a member of his family], is prohibited.

15. Flesh meat should never be eaten, not even that which remains of a sacrifice. Spirituous liquor of any kind should never be drunk, not even that presented to the Gods.

16. If an unlawful act has been committed anywhere by one's self or any other person, no member either of one's own or any other person's body should be on that account mutilated with a weapon of any kind through anger.

17. All theft is prohibited, even that which is committed under pretence of contributing to religious purposes; nor must such things as wood and flowers that have an owner ever be abstracted without his permission.

18. Let no male or female followers of mine ever commit

adultery. Let them shun gaming and similar vices, and abstain from all intoxicating liquors and substances such as hemp, etc.

19. Nowhere--except in Jagannâtha-purî--let a man accept water or food which has been cooked by one from whom food is not to be taken (ie. from a person of low caste), even though that food may have formed the Prasâda [Footnote: By Prasâda is meant the remains of food presented as an offering to a god. Here the word must be either prasâdî or prasâdi, from prasâdin] of Krishna (that is, the remains of what has been presented as an offering to Krishna).

20. No calumnious language must be used against any one for the sake of promoting one's own interests. No abusive words must ever be spoken.

21. Never use nor listen to profane language against the Gods, sacred places, Brâhmans, holy women, Sâdhus and the Vedas.

22. The remains of the offering to that Goddess to whom flesh and liquor are offered and in whose presence the killing of goats, etc., takes place, are not to be eaten.

23. If you happen on the road to see before you a temple of Śiva or any other God, having first made a salutation, respectfully enter inside to view the image.

24. Let no one abandon the duties of the class and order to which he belongs, nor practise the religious duties of others; nor have anything to do with those propounded by heretical teachers.

25. The narrative of the exploits of the Lord Krishna should not be heard from the mouth of any person whose words lead one to fall from his worship or from duty.

26. Never tell a truth which is likely to cause serious injury to yourself or to any one else. Avoid associating with ungrateful persons. Never accept a bribe from any person whatever.

27. Never associate with thieves, wicked or vicious persons, heretics, people who are in love, and people who are engaged in dishonest occupations.

28. Never associate with those who, through eager desire to obtain a wife, wealth or some sensual gratification, practise sinful acts under pretext of devotion to religion or to sacred knowledge.

29. Never pay attention to those books in which Krishna and his incarnations are impugned by controversial arguments.

30. No unstrained water or milk should be drunk, nor should water containing minute insects be used for such purposes as bathing, etc.

31. Never take medicine which is mixed with spirituous liquor or flesh meat; or which has been prescribed by a physician whose character is unknown.

32. Never allow bodily excretions or evacuations or saliva to fall in places prohibited by the Šâstras or by public custom.

33. Never enter or leave (a house) by a side entrance (or private door); never take up your residence at a place belonging to another person, without asking the owner's permission.

34. Males ought not to listen to (discourses on) religious knowledge, or to tales (about the exploits of heroes) from the mouths of women, [Footnote: This is in strict unison with the present Hindû practice of keeping women ignorant. That women in ancient times were not only educated, but sometimes

erudite and celebrated as religious teachers, is proved by the example of Maitreyî, Gârgî and others] nor ought they to carry on controversial discussions with females; nor with a king or his officials.

35. Never speak disrespectfully of religious preceptors, of superiors, of those who have gained renown in the world, of learned men, and of those that carry arms.

36. Never do any act rashly; nor be slow in a religious duty. Impart to others the knowledge you may receive, and daily associate with holy men.

37. Do not go empty-handed to pay a visit to a religious preceptor, a god or a king. Never betray a trust or violate confidence. Never praise yourself with your own lips.

38. The clothing of my followers should not be of such an improper kind that, when put on, the limbs are exposed to view.

39. The worship of Krishna must not be performed without attending to religious duties. Adoration of Krishna should not be abandoned through fear of the reproaches of ignorant people.

40. On religious festivals and on ordinary days, the males and females that go to Krishna's temple should keep separate and not touch each other.

41. Those twice-born persons who have received initiation into the worship of Krishna from a duly qualified religious teacher should always wear on their necks two rosaries made of Tulsî wood (one for Râdhâ and another for Krishna), and should make an upright mark on their foreheads.

42. This mark should be made with Gopî-çandana (ie. white

earth from Dvârikâ), or with sandal which is left from that employed in the worship of Hari (Krishna), and mixed with saffron.

43. Within this (erect mark) there ought to be made a round (vritta) mark with the materials (or earth) used for the Pundra, or with saffron which has served for the Prasâda of Râdhâ and Krishna (that is, with a portion left from that employed in their worship).

44. Those pure Šûdras who are worshippers of Krishna, while practising their own peculiar duties, should, like the twice-born, use a rosary and a vertical mark on the forehead.

45. By those (Šûdra) worshippers who are different from the pure Šûdras two rosaries made of sandal wood, etc., are to be worn on the throat, and only a round mark is to be made on the forehead.

46. Those twice-born of my followers, who have inherited from their forefathers the custom of using a rosary of Rudrâksha berries (sacred to Šiva), and the three horizontal (Šaiva) marks, should not discontinue that practice.

47. Nârâyana and Šiva should be equally regarded as manifestations of one and the same Universal Spirit, since both have been declared in the Vedas to be forms of Brahma. [Footnote: This precept furnishes an interesting proof of the tolerant character of Vaishnavism, and of its harmony with the pantheism of the Vedânta.]

48. In times of slight distress my adherents shall not chiefly (or by preference) follow the laws which are laid down by the Šâstras for times of (excessive) distress.

49. Every day let every man awake before sunrise, and after calling on the name of Krishna, proceed to the rites of bodily purification.

50. Having seated himself in some place apart, let him cleanse his teeth, and then, having bathed with pure water, put on two well-washed garments (an under and an upper).

51. Then having seated himself on a clean and single (asamkîrna) seat placed on ground purified (with cow-dung, etc.), let a man sip water with his face either to the east or north.

52. My male followers should then make the vertical mark with the round spot in it on their foreheads, and wives should only make a circular mark with red powder (of saffron).

53. A widow is prohibited from making either a vertical or round mark on her forehead. In the next place all my followers ought to engage in the mental worship of Krishna.

54. After engaging in mental worship, let them bow down before the pictures of Râdhâ and Krishna, and repeat the eight-syllabled prayer to Krishna (that is--the formula meaning 'Krishna is my refuge') as many times as possible. After that they may apply themselves to their secular affairs.

55. All my ordinary disciples should perform the preceding rules; but those who like Ambarîsha have dedicated their whole souls (to the Deity) should be most particular in performing the duties ending with mental worship in the order enumerated (in the preceding six verses as well as the following):--

56. (Such devoted persons) should also then worship an image made of either stone or metal, and the black stone called Šâla-grâma (representing Vishnu), with the (sixteen) offerings

(of sandal, etc.), such as are procurable, and the eight-syllabled mantra of Krishna should be repeated (manu = mantra).

57. Next (in order to the performance of brahma-yaj"na) the hymn celebrating the praises of Krishna should be recited according to ability, and those that have not studied Sanskrit should at least repeat his name.

58. All who have devoted themselves (in this way) to the worship of Krishna, should next present an offering (of cooked food) to him, and then they should eat the remains of the offering (prâsâdikam). They should at all times be full of joy.

59. Since they are called the passionless (nirguna) worshippers of the passionless Krishna, therefore, in consequence of that, all their acts are also (called) passionless (nirguna).

60. By these devoted (worshippers) indeed no water should be drunk, nor should any leaves, roots or fruits anywhere be eaten which have not been presented to Krishna.

61. All those who from old age or some grievous calamity are unable (to perform worship) should make over the (image or Šala-grâma stone) of Krishna to the charge of some other devotee (able to carry on the proper services), and should themselves act to the best of their ability.

62. An image (or Šâla-grâma) of Krishna, given by a religious leader (âçârya), or consecrated by him, should be worshipped, but to other images it is sufficient to make obeisance.

63. Every day all my followers should go to the temple of God in the evening, and there loudly repeat the names of the lord of Râdhikâ.

64. The story of his exploits should be related as well as heard with the greatest reverence, and on festivals hymns in praise of Krishna should be sung accompanied by musical instruments.

65. In this manner all my followers should every day perform religious duties. Moreover, they should study works both in Sanskrit and in the popular dialects, according to their mental abilities.

66. Whatever individual is appointed to any office, he should be so appointed with strict regard to his qualifications, after due consideration, and never in any other way.

67. Let every one always provide his own servants with food and clothing in the most suitable manner, and according to his own pecuniary means.

68. In conversation every person should be addressed conformably to his character (or qualities), and suitably to time and place, and not in any other manner.

69. By all well-conducted persons due deference must be shown to a religious guide, a king, an elder, an ascetic, a learned man, and one that practises austerities, by rising from the seat and so forth.

70. No man should sit down on the ground in the presence of a religious preceptor, a god, or king, or in a (solemn) assembly, in such a (disrespectful) attitude as to make one foot rest on the thigh, or with a cloth tied round the (waist and) knees.

71. A controversial discussion should never be carried on with a religious teacher (*âçârya*). He is to be honoured with gifts of food, money, clothes, and with all other things according to ability.

72. When any of my disciples hear of his arrival, they should immediately show their respect by advancing to meet him, and when he departs, they should accompany him as far as the confines of the village.

73. If an act, attended with large recompense, be opposed to religious duty, that act ought not to be committed; for religious duty (when performed) confers all desired objects.

74. An unrighteous act that may have been committed by great persons in former times must never be held (worthy of imitation); but their virtuous conduct only is to be imitated.

75. Let not the secrets of any one be ever anywhere divulged, the neglect (vyatikrama) of proper respect (for those deserving of reverence) should never be made, (as if all were to be looked at) with an equal eye (of esteem).

76. All my disciples should practise special religious observances during the four special months (beginning with Âshâdha). But those who are sickly need only practise the same in the one month of Šrâvana only.

77. Reading and listening to the exploits of Vishnu, singing his praises, solemn worship, repetition of his mantra ("Great Krishna is my refuge"), recitation of the hymn of praise (ie. of the thousand names of Vishnu), reverential circumambulations (from left to right with the right side towards the object adored),

78. Prostration with the eight members (of the body) these are considered the best religious observances; any one of these ought to be performed with special devotion.

79. The fasts of all the eleventh days (of the waxing and waning moon) should be carefully observed; also of the birthdays of

Krishna; and of the night of Śiva (*Śiva-râtri*) with rejoicings during the day.

80. On a fast-day sleeping by day should most carefully be avoided, since by such sleep the merit of fasting is lost to men, quite as much as by sexual intercourse.

81. Whatever appointed order of religious fasts and festivals (vrata and utsava) was enjoined by Śrî Viththaleša (Viththalanatha), who was the son of Śrî Vallabhâçârya, the most eminent of Vaishnavas.

82. Having conformed to that order, all religious fasts and festivals should be observed accordingly; and the form of worshipping Krishna directed by him (Viththaleša) should be adopted.

83. A pilgrimage to the Tîrthas, or holy places, of which Dvârikâ (Krishna's city in Gujarât) is the chief, should be performed according to rule. Love and Charity should be shown towards the poor by all, according to ability.

84. Vishnu, Śiva, Gana-pati (Ganeša), Pârvatî, and the Sun, these five deities should be honoured with worship by my followers. [Footnote: It is evident from this verse, as from verse 47, that although Vaishnavas give preferential worship to Vishnu, they are really Pantheists in the sense of honouring other deities, as manifestations of the Supreme Being. It may be observed that although five deities are here mentioned, Ganapati and Pârvatî are connected with Śiva, as the Sun is with Vishnu.]

85. When at any place a calamity is caused by a demon or by any similar cause, the charm called Nârâyana should be recited or the mantra of Hanumân should be muttered, but not the mantra of any inferior god less esteemed.

86. On the occurrence of eclipses of the sun and moon, all my followers should immediately suspend their other business, and, having purified themselves, should make repetition of the (eight-syllabled) mantra of Krishna.

87. When the eclipse has passed off, they should bathe with their clothes on, and those who are householders should distribute gifts according to their ability. Other persons (who have no worldly means) should engage in the worship of the supreme Lord (Vishnu).

88. Those followers of mine who belong to the four classes should observe, in conformity with the Šâstras, the rules in regard to the contraction of impurity through births and deaths, according to the degree of kinship.

89. Brâhmans should possess tranquillity of mind, self-restraint, forbearance, contentment and similar virtues. Kshatriyas (or the soldier caste) should be remarkable for bravery, fortitude, and the like qualities.

90. Vaišyas (or the agricultural and commercial caste) should occupy themselves in mercantile pursuits, money-lending, and the like. Šûdras (or the servile class) should be employed in serving the twice-born, etc.

91. The twice-born should perform at the proper seasons, and according to their means--each according to his own domestic rules--the twelve purificatory rites [Footnote: Of these only six are now generally performed, viz.:--1, the birth-ceremony, or touching the tongue of a new-born infant with clarified butter, etc.; 2, the name-giving ceremony on the tenth day; 3, tonsure; 4, induction into the privileges of the twice-born, by investiture with the sacred thread; 5, solemn return home from the house of a preceptor after completing the prescribed course of study; 6,

marriage. See *Indian Wisdom*, p. 246.] (*sanskâra*), the (six) daily duties [Footnote: The six daily duties (called Nitya-karman), according to Parâśara, are:--1, bathing; 2, morning and evening prayer (sandhyâ); 3, repetition of sacred texts; 4, offerings to fire (homa); 5, worship of ancestors; 6, worship of the gods. The six daily acts enjoined by Manu are different. See *Indian Wisdom*, p. 244.], and the Śraddha offerings to the spirits of departed ancestors.

92. If intentionally or unintentionally any sin, great or small, be committed, the proper penance must be performed according to ability.

93. The Vedas, the Vedânta-sûtras of Vyasa, the Bhâgavata-purâna and the thousand names of Vishnu in the Mahâbhârata,

94. The Bhagavad-gîtâ and the precepts of Vidura, the Vâsudeva-mâhâtmya from the Vaishnava-khan.da of the Skanda-Purâna,

95. And the Smriti of Yâj"navalkya, which is one of the Dharma-Śâstras, these eight sacred books are approved by me as authorities. [Footnote: I commend this list to the attention of those European scholars who wish to be guided by Indian authorities in determining the real "sacred books" of India.]

96. All my twice-born disciples who wish good to themselves should recite these sacred books and hear them recited.

97. In deciding questions of ancient usage (âçara), or practice, or penance, the code of Yâj"navalkya, with its commentary the Mitâksharâ, should be taken (as the best authority).

98. The tenth and fifth books of the Bhâgavata Purâna are to be regarded as having the preeminence over all the other sacred

books for the understanding of the glory of Krishna.

99. The tenth and fifth books of the Bhâgavata Purâna and the code of Yâj"navalkya are respectively my Bhakti-šâstra (manual of faith), Yoga-šâstra (manual of devotion), and Dharma-šâstra (manual of law).

100. As a treatise on the soul, the commentary on the Bhagavad-Gîtâ as well as that on the Šârîraka-Sûtras of Vyâsa, made by Râmânujâçârya, commends itself to my approval.

101. Whatever precepts in these sacred books have for their subject the excessive exaltation of Krishna and of Justice (V.risha), of faith and of indifference to the world--

102. Such precepts should be regarded as taking precedence over all others. Their essential doctrine is that devotion to Krishna should be joined with the performance of duty.

103. Duty (*dharma*) is that good practice which is enjoined both by the Veda (Šruti) and by the law (Smriti) founded on the Veda. Devotion (*bhakti*) is intense love for Krishna, accompanied with a due sense of his glory.

104. Indifference to worldly objects means absence of satisfaction in any object except Krishna. True knowledge consists in discriminating rightly between the nature of the personal soul (jiva), of the external world (Mâyâ), and of the Supreme Being (Îša).

105. The personal soul dwells in the heart. It is as subtle as an atom; it is all thought; it has the faculty of knowledge; it is ascertained to be constantly pervading the whole body (ie. the three corporeal envelopes kârana, sûkshma, and sthûla) by its power of perception; it is characterized by indivisibility

and the like.

106. The external world (Mâyâ) is identical with the energizing power of Krishna. It is composed of the three Gunas; it is darkness; it is to be understood as the cause of the soul's having such ideas in regard to the body, and the things relating to the body, as are conveyed by the expressions I, mine, and the like.

107. He who abides in the living personal soul in the character of an internal monitor, as the personal soul dwells in the heart, he is to be considered as the Self-existent Supreme Being, the Rewarder of all actions.

108. That Being, known by various names--such as the glorious Krishna, Param Brahma, Bhagavân, Purushottamah-- the cause of all manifestations, is to be adored by us as our one chosen deity.

109. He, together with Râdhâ, should be regarded as the Supreme Lord, under the name of Râdhâ-Krishna. With Rukminî and Ramâ he is known as Lakshmî-Nârâyana.

110. When joined with Arjuna, he is known by the name of Nara-Nârâyana; when associated with Bala-bhadra (= Bala-râma), or any other divine personage, he is called Râmâ-Krishna and so on.

111. Those devoted (female companions of the god) Râdhâ and his other (consorts) are in some places represented at his side. In other places (their images do not appear, because) they are supposed to be one with his body and he with theirs.

112. On no account let it be supposed that difference in forms makes any difference in the identity of the deity. For the two-armed Krishna may exhibit himself with four arms (or eight, or

a thousand, or any number of arms).

113. Towards him alone ought all faith and worship (bhakti) to be directed by every human being on earth in every possible manner. Nothing else, except such (faith), is able to procure salvation.

114. The best result of the virtues of those who possess good qualities is faith in Krishna and association with holy men; without these, even persons who know (the Šâstras) go downwards (towards a lower state).

115. Meditation should be directed towards Krishna, his incarnations and their images, but not towards living men, nor (inferior) gods, etc., nor devotees, nor (even) those who (merely) have knowledge of Brahma.

116. Having perceived, by abstract meditation, that the Spirit or Self is distinct from its three bodies (viz. the gross, subtle and causal bodies), and that it is a portion of the one Spirit of the Universe (Brahma), every man ought to worship Krishna by means of that (self) at all times.

117. The tenth book of the Bhâgavata-Purâna should be listened to reverentially, and learned men should read it daily or (if frequent reading is impossible, at least) once a year.

118. The repetition (of the Bhâgavata), as well as of the thousand names of Vishnu, etc., should be performed as far as possible in a pure place (such as the precincts of a temple); for (such repetition) causes the accomplishment of desired objects.

119. On the occurrence of any disaster caused by the elements (such as a flood or fire), or when any human calamity or sickness takes place, a man should be wholly occupied in striving to

preserve himself and other people and in nothing else.

120. Religious usages, business transactions and penances, should be adapted to country, time, age, property, rank and ability.

121. The (philosophical) doctrine approved by me is the Višishtâdvaita (of Râmânuja) [Footnote: This verse proves that in their philosophical ideas the Svâmi-Nârâyana sect are followers of the Râmânuja sect. Compare verse 100.], and the desired heavenly abode is Goloka. There to worship Krishna, and be united with him as the Supreme Soul of the Universe, is to be considered salvation (Mukti).

122. These that have been specified are the general duties, applicable to all my followers, whether male or female. Now I am about to enumerate the special duties.

123. The two sons of my elder and younger brothers (viz. Ayodhyâ-prasâda and Raghu-vîra) ought never to impart instruction to any women except their nearest relations.

124. They ought never to touch or converse with any women in any place whatever. Cruelty should never be shown towards any person. A deposit belonging to another should never be taken charge of.

125. In business matters no one should stand security for any other person. In passing through a time of distress it is right to ask for alms, but debts should not be contracted.

126. One should not sell corn bestowed by one's own disciples; having given away old corn, new corn is to be bought. That is not called a sale.

127. On the fourth day of the light-half of the month Bhâdra, the worship of Ganeśa should be performed, and on the fourteenth of the dark-half of Âśvina, Hanumân should be worshipped.

128. Those two sons (of my brothers, viz. Ayodhyâ-prasâda and Raghu-vîra), who have been appointed as spiritual guides to guard the religious interests of my followers, should initiate all desirous of obtaining salvation (in the use of the mantra of Krishna).

129. They should cause each of their disciples to continue steadfast in his own appointed duty. Honour should be paid to holy men, and the sacred Śâstras should be reverently repeated.

130. Worship of Lakshmî-Nârâyana, and other forms of Krishna that have been set up and consecrated by me in the great temples, should be performed with the proper ceremonies.

131. Any one who may come to the temple of Krishna to ask for a gift of food (cooked or uncooked) should be received with respect, and food given to him according to ability.

132. Having established a school for giving instruction, some learned Brâhman should be appointed over it. True knowledge should be promoted throughout the world, for that is an act of great merit.

133. The two wives of these (sons of my brothers), with the permission of their respective husbands, should initiate females only (eva) in the Mantra of Krishna.

134. They should never touch or speak to other males than their nearest relations; nor should they ever show their faces to them.

135. My male followers who are householders should never

touch widows unless they are their own near relatives.

136. They should not remain alone in any private place with a youthful mother, sister or daughter, except in a time of distress. Nor should a wife be given away (to another man).

137. No attachment should on any account be formed with a woman who in any transactions has been brought into connexion with the king of the country.

138. When a guest has arrived at a house, he should be honoured by those (who live in it) with food and other things according to ability. Offerings to the Gods and the Pitris (at the Devatâ-tarpana and Pitri-tarpana and Šrâddha ceremonies) should be made according to right usage and according to one's means.

139. It is the duty of my disciples, as long as they live and according to their ability, to honour with faithful attention their father, mother, spiritual preceptor, and any one affected with sickness.

140. Every person should, according to his ability, carry on some occupation suitable to his caste and religious order. Those that live by agriculture should not allow a bull to be gelded.

141. Provisions and money should be laid by according to circumstances and time; and those that keep cattle should store up as much hay as these animals may need for their consumption.

142. If a man can himself attend to the proper feeding of cows and other animals with hay and water, then only he may keep them, otherwise he must not do so.

143. No business in regard to giving or receiving land or

property should ever be transacted even with a son or friend, without a written deed attested by witnesses.

144. When any pecuniary transactions connected with giving away a girl in marriage have to be transacted for one's self or another person, the money to be delivered over should not be settled by verbal agreement, but only by a written contract attested by witnesses.

145. A man's expenditure ought always to be in proportion to his income. Otherwise it is certain that great misery will arise.

146. Every day one should take note of one's income and expenditure in the regular business of life, and write them down with one's own hand.

147. My followers should assign a tithe of the grain, money, etc., acquired by their own occupation or exertions, to Krishna, and the poor should give a twentieth part.

148. The due performance of fasts, of which the eleventh-day fasts are the principal, should be effected according to the Šâstras and one's ability; for this will lead to the attainment of desired objects.

149. Every year in the month Šrâvana one should perform, or cause others to perform, cheerfully the worship of Šiva with the leaves of the Bilva-tree, etc.

150. Neither money, nor utensils, nor ornaments, nor clothes should be borrowed for use (on festive occasions) from one's own spiritual preceptor, or from the temple of Krishna.

151. While going to do homage to great Krishna, to a spiritual preceptor, or to a holy man, food should not be accepted from

others on the road, or at the places of pilgrimage; for such food takes away religious merit.

152. The full amount of promised wages should be paid to a workman. Payment of a debt is never to be kept secret. Let no one have any dealings with wicked men.

153. If through great distress caused by a famine, by enemies, or by (the oppression of) a king, any danger of destruction arises anywhere to character, wealth or life,

154. The wise among my followers should at once quit even their own native country, and having gone to another, let them reside there happily.

155. Wealthy householders should perform those sacrifices in honour of Vishnu which entail no killing of animals. Brâhmans and holy men (Sâdhus) should be fed on festival days at sacred places of pilgrimage.

156. They should observe the great festivals in honour of the Deity in the temples, and should distribute various gifts among Brâhmans who are deserving objects (of generosity).

157. Kings who are my followers should govern all their subjects in accordance with the law (laid down in the Dharma-šâstras), and should protect them as if they were their children, and should establish the observance of proper duties throughout the whole land.

158. They should be well acquainted with the circumstances of their kingdom; as, for example, with the seven Angas (viz. the duties of the sovereign, minister, ally, treasury, territory, fortresses and army); the four Upâyas (viz. conciliation, sowing dissension, bribing, and punishing); the six Gunas (viz. peace,

war, marching, sitting encamped, dividing the forces, having recourse to an ally for protection); and the places of resort to which spies should be sent. They should also make themselves acquainted with the men who are skilled in legal procedure, and with all the court functionaries, observing by the right signs whether any ought to be punished or not. [Footnote: With reference to this verse compare Manu's directions to Kings (Books vii. and viii.), and the precepts in the Vigraha chapter of the Hitopadeša.]

159. Wives should honour their husbands as if they were gods, and never offend them with improper language, though they be diseased, indigent, or imbecile. [Footnote: Compare Manu, v. 154.]

160. No communication, even though arising naturally (*sâhajika*), should be held with any other man who may be possessed of beauty, youth and good qualities.

161. A chaste woman should not allow her navel, thighs, or breasts to be seen by males; nor should she remain without an upper garment (anuttarîyâ), nor should she look at (the antics of) buffoons, nor associate with an immodest woman.

162. A wife while her husband is absent in a foreign country should wear neither ornaments nor fine clothes; she ought not to frequent other people's houses, and should abstain from laughing and talking with other women.

163. Widows should serve the God Krishna with minds intent on him as their only husband; they should live under the control of their father, or other male members of the family, and never in independence.

164. They must never at any time touch any men except their

nearest relations, and when young they should never without necessity engage in conversation with youthful men.

165. If an infant male-child touch them, no blame attaches to them, any more than from contact with a dumb animal; nor if they are compelled from necessity to talk with or touch an old man.

166. Instruction in any science should not be received by them from any man except from their nearest relations. They should frequently emaciate their bodies by vows and fasts.

167. They should never give away to others the money which is required for their own support. That only must be given away which they have in excess.

168. They should eat only one meal a day, and should sleep on the ground; they should never look at (animals) engaged in sexual acts.

169. They must never wear the dress of a married woman, nor of a female ascetic, nor of a mendicant, nor any unbecoming attire.

170. They should neither associate with nor touch a woman who has been guilty of procuring abortion; nor should they either converse about, or hear stories of the loves of the male sex.

171. Except in times of distress widows who are young should never remain alone in secret places along with men, even with their own relatives, if youthful.

172. They should never join in the frolics practised at the Holî festival, nor should they put on ornaments or finely woven clothes composed of cotton or metal threads.

173. Neither wives nor widows ought ever to bathe without

wearing clothes. No woman should ever conceal the first appearance of her monthly periods.

174. A woman at that season should not for an interval of three days touch any human being, clothes, etc.; nor ought she to do so till she has bathed on the fourth day.

175. Those of my followers who have taken the vow of Naishthika Brahmaçârîs (that is, of perpetual celibacy and chastity) must not knowingly either touch or converse with or look at women.

176. They should never talk or listen to conversations about women, and they should not perform their ablutions or other religious rites at places where women pass backwards and forwards.

177. They should never knowingly touch or look at even the pictures or wooden images of women, unless they be the representations of goddesses.

178. They should neither draw any likeness of a woman, nor touch her clothes. They must never knowingly look even at animals engaged in sexual acts.

179. They should neither touch nor look at a male dressed up as a woman; nor should they sing the praises of the Deity with a view to being heard by women.

180. They should pay no attention to the command of even their spiritual preceptor if likely to lead them to a breach of their vow of chastity. They should continue steadfast, contented, and humble-minded.

181. When a woman insists on forcing herself near them, they

should immediately try to keep her off by expostulating with her, and (if she still approaches) by reproaching her.

182. In cases where their own lives, or those of women, are in jeopardy, they may be allowed contact or conversation with women, such contact being necessary for the saving of life.

183. They should not anoint their lips with oil. They should not carry weapons. They should not dress themselves in unbecoming costume. They should subdue the sense of taste.

184. If in the house of any Brâhman the meals are cooked and served up by a woman, they should not go there to ask for food, but should ask for it at some other house.

185. They should constantly repeat the Vedas and Šâstras, and serve their spiritual preceptor. They must shun the society of women, and of men who are fond of women.

186. He who is by birth a Brâhman should on no account drink water from a leathern vessel; nor should he ever eat garlic, onions, etc.

187. Nor must he eat food without having first performed his ablutions, the Sandhyâ service, repetition of the Gâyatri, the worship of Vishnu, and the Vaišvadeva ceremony. [Footnote: This ceremony, which partly consists in throwing portions of food into the fire, before dinner, as an offering to all the deities, will be fully described in my new work on "Religious Thought and Life in India," to be published by Mr. Murray.]

188. All who are Sâdhus are bound, just like those who have made a vow of perpetual celibacy, to avoid associating with women, or with men who are fond of women, and should subdue their (six) internal enemies (lust, anger, avarice, infatuation,

pride, and envy).

189. They should subjugate all the senses, more especially the sense of taste; they should neither lay by a store of property themselves, nor make others do so for them.

190. They must not take charge of any one's deposit, they should never relax their firmness, nor allow a woman to enter their abodes at any time. [Footnote: We may notice that there is no little repetition in this Book of instructions, especially in enforcing the duty of keeping clear of all feminine seductions.]

191. Except at a time of distress, they should never go anywhere by night without a companion, nor should they travel to any place singly.

192. They should not use a costly variegated cloth, or one dyed with kusumbha, or dyed in any other way; or any expensive cloth, though freely presented to them by another.

193. They should not go to the houses of householders unless for the purpose of asking alms, or for being present at an assembly. They should not spend time uselessly without devoting any of it to the worship of the Deity.

194. To the abode of a householder in which only males are employed for serving up the cooked food, and where no woman is to be seen--

195. To the house of such a householder only should my Sâdhus resort for participation in a meal, otherwise they should ask for uncooked food, and prepare it themselves.

196. All my holiest sages should conduct themselves in the same manner as Bharata, son of .Rishabha, the idiot Brâhman

(Jada-vipra), did in ancient times. [Footnote: The story is told in Vishnu-purâna, ii. 13. He feigned idiocy, that he might not be troubled with worldly society and might so give his undivided attention to devotional exercises.]

197. Those holy men (Sâdhus) who are Brahmaçârîs should diligently abstain from eating or using betel-leaves, opium, tobacco (tamâla), etc.

198. They should never accept a meal given on the performance of the Sanskâra ceremonies, beginning with that of conception; [Footnote: See note to verse 91.] nor on performing the Šrâddha ceremony at death, nor at that performed on the 12th day after decease.

199. They should never sleep during the day, unless afflicted with sickness, etc. They should never gossip about local matters, nor intentionally listen to such gossip.

200. They should not lie down on a bedstead except when suffering from illness or other affliction, and should be guileless and straightforward in their behaviour towards other Sâdhus.

201. They should patiently bear abusive language, or even blows from evil-minded persons, and wish good to (them in return).

202. They should not undertake the work of a go-between or informer, or spy; they should never show selfishness or partiality towards their relations.

203. Thus I have specified in a summary manner the general duties of all. Those who desire more particular instructions must refer to the sacred books handed down by tradition.

204. Having myself extracted the essence of an the sacred

Šâstrâs, I have written this Directory, which leads men to the attainment of desired objects.

205. Hence it is incumbent on my followers, having their minds well controlled, to conduct themselves in conformity with its precepts, and not according to their own wills.

206. Those males and females of my disciples who will act according to these directions shall certainly obtain the four great objects of human desires (viz. *Dharma*, religious merit; *Artha*, wealth; *Kâma*, pleasure; and *Moksha*, final beatitude).

207. Those who will not act according to these (directions) shall be considered by my male and female followers as excluded from communion with my sect.

208. My followers should daily read this Book of directions, and those who do not know how to read should listen to others reading it.

209. But in the absence of a reader (vaktrabhâve), worship should be paid to it every day, and it should be honoured with the greatest reverence as my word and my representative.

210. This Directory should only be given to those persons who are endowed with a nature of the divine type; never to a man possessing a nature of the demoniacal type. [Footnote: The Purânas divide all men into two classes: those whose nature is divine, and those whose nature is demoniacal.]

211. This Book of directions, bringing welfare (to all who study it), was completed on the first day of the season of spring in the year 1882 of the era of Vikramâditya. (= A.D. 1826).

212. May Krishna, the remover of the sufferings of his

worshippers, the maintainer of devotion, accompanied with the performance of proper duties, the bestower of the desires of the heart, grant us blessings of all kinds!

www.ingramcontent.com/pod-product-compliance
Lightning Source LLC
Chambersburg PA
CBHW022125090426
42743CB00008B/1017